A Magical Racquet Ride

JOURNEY TO THE FOUR GRAND SLAM TOURNAMENTS OF TENNIS

by Marissa Irvin Gould

Illustrated by Mark Brayer

Acknowledgements

A special thank you to members of the International Tennis Federation and the Grand Slam Committee, the All England Lawn Tennis Club, Tennis Australia, the Fédération Française de Tennis (French Tennis Federation), and the United States Tennis Association for their support of this project, as well as their willingness to promote the great sport of tennis by allowing the use of their trademarked Grand Slam tournament names in this children's book.

Please note that the term "Grand Slam" is a registered trademark of GSTP Ltd. and it is with the permission of GSTP that it is used within this book. "Wimbledon" is a registered trademark of the All England Lawn Tennis Club and it is with their permission that it is used within this book. "Australian Open" is a registered trademark of Tennis Australia and it is with their permission that it is used within this book. "Roland-Garros" is a registered trademark of the Fédération Française de Tennis and it is with their permission that it is used within this book. "US Open" and the "USTA Billie Jean King National Tennis Center" are registered trademarks of the United States Tennis Association and it is with their permission that they are used within this book.

Patrick, Patrick, Jr., Grace, and Mary—I love you! Nick and Molly, thank you for allowing me to use your namesakes as the magical racquet riders, and to my three kids and many students, thank you for inspiring this journey.

Cheers!

Text copyright © 2014 by Marissa Gould

Cover illustrations and interior illustrations by Mark Brayer

Library of Congress Cataloging-in-Publication Data

ISBN-13: 978-1492177081

ISBN-10: 1492177083

Published in the United States of America, First Edition

Books are available in quantity for promotional or premium use.

Visit www.amagicalracquetride.com

A Magical Racquet Ride

JOURNEY TO THE FOUR GRAND SLAM TOURNAMENTS OF TENNIS

To Amazing Ainsley who loves
tennis, adventure and her brother,
Jack! With love,
Ms. Courtney

by Marissa Irvin Gould
Illustrated by Mark Brayer

Nick and Molly blew out their candles—every last one
To a round of applause after their birthday song was done.
The presents were many; there were clothes, toys, and shoes,
But they each had a favorite, if you asked them to choose.

Two shiny new tennis racquets stood out from the rest,
Their glistening frames surely made them the best.

The twins loved sports and thought that they knew them all,
But they'd never played this sport with a racquet and fuzzy yellow ball.
When their friends all left and nighttime came,
Nick and Molly dressed for bed and lay down with their frames.

And as they dozed off, they could suddenly fly—
Sitting on their racquets, jetting through the sky!
Were they dreaming? Was this real? Nick and Molly didn't know.
Their racquets zoomed forward, knowing just where to go.

As they looked down, they saw in the sea,
A mighty statue known fondly as Lady Liberty.
There were buildings aplenty in the Empire State,
Over bridges and parks, they arrived at the gates.

There it was! A giant stadium—the largest they'd seen,

And a sign that said this center was named...for a King?

The home of the US Open, where legends are made,

Nick and Molly were in awe and ready to play!

There were straight white lines on blue and green cement,

And a net down the middle for each tennis event.

Singles and doubles for girls and for boys,

A can of three balls popped open with joy.

The twins learned that tennis is played on a court,

Not a field or a diamond like some other sports.

And terms like *baseline* and *service line*, *doubles alleys* too,

Serve and *return* and rubber-soled shoes.

Nick and Molly were excited, they loved learning new things,

But the time had come to sit back on their strings.

In the distance the twins saw the green British Isles,

As they magically traveled thousands of miles.

Over a mighty ocean, to the "granddaddy of them all."

History says England's where they struck that first tennis ball.

A queen, a palace, London Bridge, and alas—
Tennis courts made out of bright green grass?

The lines and the net, they looked just the same.

The surface was different, but not the rules of the game.

Fifteen, thirty, forty, deuce,

And love means nothing? Wow, this was new!

Wimbledon is special and full of tradition,

Just to walk on the courts required special permission.

Nick and Molly wore shoes with tiny little nubby spikes,

They ate strawberries and cream, and their clothes
had to be white.

Their time in Great Britain sadly came to an end,

So the twins hopped aboard and said, "Cheerio," to Big Ben.

Over the English Channel and onward to France,

Nick and Molly beamed with glee and did a happy dance.

The Eiffel Tower and the Louvre (on the ground below),

Notre Dame, Versailles, and then their rides began to slow.

The twins landed in Paris and saw courts of red

With the name "Roland-Garros" and new berets on their heads?

Here, tennis was played on a surface called clay.

In France, it's crushed bricks; that's what the locals say.

You run and slide as you hit your next shot;

Forehands and *backhands*—they were learning a lot!

It's dusty and dirty but as fun as can be.

Game, set, match—now, "Au revoir, Paris!"

On the other side of the world, in "the land down under,"

Nick and Molly found themselves toward the end of their

slumber.

They saw kangaroos in the outback and koalas in the trees,
The famed Sydney Opera House, and the Great Barrier Reef.

At Melbourne Park, their racquets finally stopped;

Onto a squishy blue court they quickly did hop.

The site of the Australian Open, the first Grand Slam.

Tennis has four championships? This sport is quite glam!

Two out of three sets or three out of five,

And after every other game, the players switched sides.

They learned how to *volley* and smash an *overhead*,

Then all of a sudden...

They were back in their beds!

The twins woke to the sound of their mom's loving voice,

"Breakfast time, kids; eggs or toast—it's your choice!"

Still holding their racquets, Nick and Molly slowly rose;

It must have been a dream, and then...

They froze.

Just beside their pillows, resting on their beds,

Was proof the adventure hadn't been in their heads:

There sat their fabulous, floppy, French berets...

"Mom! We have something we want to share at school today!"

About the Author

Marissa Irvin Gould is a mother of three, professional tennis player, and elementary school teacher. She played on the WTA tour, appearing in twenty-two Grand Slam events during her career, and has won professional tournaments in singles and doubles, was an NCAA champion, a four-time collegiate All-American, and a US National junior champion. Mrs. Gould holds a Bachelor of Arts degree in political science from Stanford University as well as a Master's degree in education from Pepperdine University and a California teaching credential. She has taught both kindergarten and third grade; however, since having her first child in 2008, Mrs. Gould has put away the lesson plans while she is home with her three young children. She enjoys spending her days with her husband and family near their home in California, and hopes every child will have the opportunity to discover the magic of tennis.

44016103R00020

Made in the USA
Middletown, DE
25 May 2017